WITHDRAWN

EDGE
BOOKS

STEAM JOBS
FOR
WORKERS WILLING TO
GET DIRTY

BY SAM RHODES

raintree

a Capstone company — publishers for children

Raintree is an imprint of Capstone Global Library Limited, a company incorporated in England and Wales having its registered office at 264 Banbury Road, Oxford, OX2 7DY – Registered company number: 6695582

www.raintree.co.uk
myorders@raintree.co.uk

Lauren Dupuis-Perez, editor; Sara Radka, designer; Kathy McColley, production specialist

ISBN 978 1 4747 6412 4 (hardback)
22 21 20 19 18
10 9 8 7 6 5 4 3 2 1

British Library Cataloguing in Publication Data
A full catalogue record for this book is available from the British Library.

Acknowledgements
Getty Images: AF-studio, background, AlpamayoPhoto, 29 (top), amana images, 7 (top), ARS, 29 (bottom), bdspn, cover (back), Caiaimage, 8, Chris Sattlberger, 20, Daniel LeClair, 26, DmyTo, 9 (bottom), heyjojo19, 14, iznashih, 25 (left), lucentius, 28, Matt Cardy, 16, Ron Levine, 11 (bottom), salajean, 22, Savany, cover (front), stockdevil, 27 (top), Susana Gonzalez, 18, Thorney Lieberman, 11 (top); Newscom: BELMONTE/BSIP, 6, MCT/Dallas Morning News/Sonya N. Hebert, 7 (bottom), Peter & Georgina Bowater Stock Connection Worldwide, 4, Solent News/Melih Sular, 10, ZUMA Wire/TASS/Dmitry Rogulin, 24; Pixabay: snarlingbunny, 1; Shutterstock: Alaattin Timur, 23, Andriy Blokhin, 17, Avatar_023, 21, ChameleonsEye, 15 (bottom), Couperfield, 12, kamnuan, 15 (top), LeitWolf, 9 (top), paleontologist natural, 27 (bottom), Polina Petrenko, 25 (right), SGr, 19, Vitalii Hulai, 13 (bottom), Worraket, 13 (top)

Every effort has been made to contact copyright holders of material reproduced in this book. Any omissions will be rectified in subsequent printings if notice is given to the publisher.

All the Internet addresses (URLs) given in this book were valid at the time of going to press. However, due to the dynamic nature of the Internet, some addresses may have changed, or sites may have changed or ceased to exist since publication. While the author and publisher regret any inconvenience this may cause readers, no responsibility for any such changes can be accepted by either the author or the publisher.

Printed and bound in India.

CONTENTS

INTRODUCTION
DIRT, MUD AND SLIME

An oil drill operator's day-to-day tasks, such as withdrawing a drill bit from the drill column, can get very messy.

Dirt, mud and slime are things most people avoid. But some people do not mind getting dirty. They work on their own cars and don't mind getting covered in oil and grime. They love hiking through the woods and get excited when they find interesting bugs, animal tracks and even animal droppings. These people usually love adventure and the outdoors. This willingness to get dirty can lead to some very exciting careers.

Some of the dirtiest jobs around are in STEAM-related fields. STEAM stands for science, technology, engineering, the arts and maths. Whether it is climbing into caves, drilling deep into the earth, or cleaning hazardous waste, these workers are diving in and getting the job done.

CHAPTER 1
GASTROENTEROLOGISTS

Do you giggle when people fart, instead of being digusted?
Can you walk past vomit without gagging? Vomit, farts
and burps all come from the digestive system. Body parts
in this system include the **oesophagus**, stomach, intestines
and colon. Gastroenterologists are doctors who focus on the
digestive system.

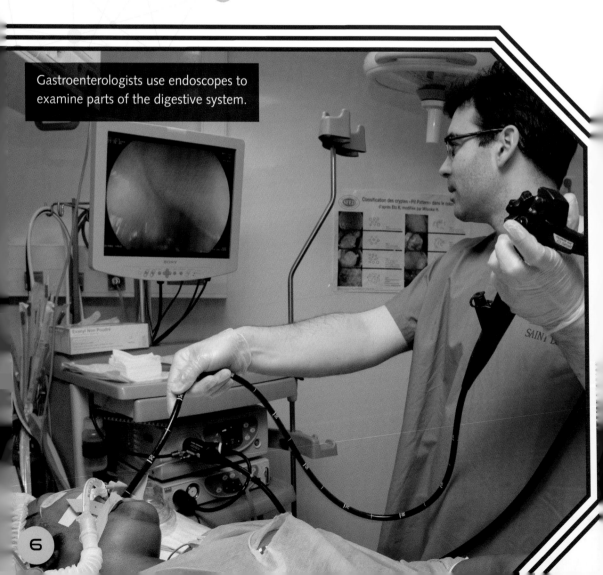

Gastroenterologists use endoscopes to
examine parts of the digestive system.

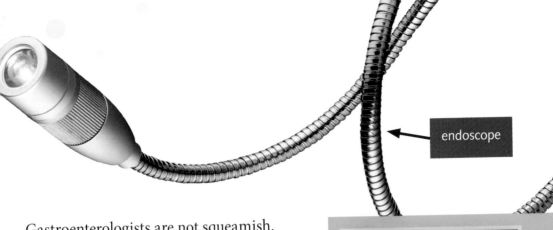

endoscope

Gastroenterologists are not squeamish. A typical day involves blood, **stools**, vomit, gas and bad breath. Sometimes gastroenterologists have to perform **rectal** exams with their fingers to see if the muscles are working correctly. They perform endoscopies and colonoscopies. Endoscopies involve putting a **scope** into a patient's mouth, down the throat and into the stomach. Colonoscopies involve placing a scope into a patient's anus to examine the colon and intestines.

Gastroenterologists also may respond to emergency calls. They help patients with serious rectal bleeding, rectal or abdominal pain, fevers and stool leakage.

EDUCATION

Success as a gastroenterologist requires a strong background in:

- **biology**
- **chemistry**
- **internal medicine**

oesophagus long tube that carries food from the mouth to the stomach

stools bodily waste that comes out of the anus

rectal having to do with the rectum, the tube that releases solid waste

scope tool a doctor uses to listen to or see inside a person's body

Miners use heavy-duty machines that kick up clouds of dust and dirt on the job site.

CONSTRUCTING THE MINE

Enormous shovels bite into the earth, then swivel, dropping the loads into dump trucks. Once full, these giant dump trucks haul earth and rock from the mine. The exhaust from the vehicles mixes with the dirt from the loose earth. A thick, dusty haze covers the open-pit mine. It also settles on a mining engineer who is watching the mining and making reports.

THE BELAZ 75710

The Belaz 75710 is the largest dump truck in the world. It is 8.1 metres (26.7 feet) tall, 20.6 m (67.5 feet) long and 9.9 m (32.4 feet) wide. It weighs 360,000 kilograms (793,664 pounds). That is about as much as 100 adult elephants!

The Belaz was designed to haul loose rock out of mines. It can carry 408,233 kg (992,080 pounds) of rock in a single load. Two enormous 16-cylinder engines power this huge truck. Most trucks have one 8-cylinder engine.

Mining engineers work with companies looking for new places to build mines. The mining engineers explore mineral-rich areas and work with **geologists** to find a good location. They study geological maps to choose a location likely to have a large amount of deposits.

When the location and type of mine is decided, the mining engineer designs the mine. Mining engineers use computer software to plan out the mine. The software allows engineers to make a digital 3-D model of the mine.

Next, the mine construction gets underway. A mining engineer oversees this process at the mining site. Underground mines can be very dirty and dusty. Masks protect mining engineers from inhaling dangerous particles while inspecting the mine. Hard hats protect them from falling rocks and equipment.

geologist person who studies rocks

MAINTAINING THE MINE

During production, mining engineers closely record what is happening. They make and update detailed maps of mines. The mining engineers sometimes go deep underground. They use special **surveying** equipment to take measurements, such as length, depth and mineral content of the mine. They also gather mineral samples from within the mine. The engineers test the samples to see if they contain valuable materials. This information tells the mining engineers where they should dig.

Mining engineers also supervise salt mines, which are usually dug into mountains.

surveying measuring land in order to make a plan for how to use it

Some of the deepest coal mines in the United States are more than 300 m (1,000 feet) underground.

Mining engineers take a hands-on approach to make sure the mine is running well. Mining engineers perform weekly inspections. They review mine equipment such as pumps, conveyor belts, fans and mine shaft lifts. That means living near the mine and making regular visits inside it. Even walking into a mine covers mining engineers with dirt and grime. Sometimes they climb up into tight spaces or crawl through small openings to inspect equipment. They might open up machines and see how engines are running. Mining engineers also inspect dirty ropes to make sure they are not worn or weak.

EDUCATION

Success as a mining engineer requires a strong background in:

- **engineering**
- **physics**
- **earth science**

CHAPTER 3

FORENSIC ENTOMOLOGISTS

The smell leaves no doubt about the location of the crime scene. Investigators are crammed into the tiny flat. A dead body lies on the kitchen floor. The crime clearly happened a long time ago. But how long? It is time to call in a professional.

Forensic entomologists are scientists who study insects that live in **decomposing** bodies. As soon as death occurs, a body begins to break down and release gases. The gases attract insects. The insects provide information about the time and place of death. But to get this information, a forensic entomologist studies gruesome scenes, complete with blood, decomposing flesh, maggots and foul smells.

Forensic entomologists have to carefully collect larvae from crime scenes.

blow fly larvae

Forensic entomologists help police investigate mysterious deaths. These specialists go to crime scenes to take photographs and collect samples. They use their insect knowledge to establish time of death based on **larvae** growth and damage to the body. These scientists also determine if insects present in a victim were from the location where a body was found or if the insects came from another area. This information tells investigators if the body was moved.

Forensic entomologists review photos and crime-scene samples in labs. They study partially decomposed tissue samples, insects and insect eggs that are present. Based on the evidence, they write reports to be used in court. They also may be asked to talk about their findings in court.

EDUCATION

Success as a forensic entomologist requires a strong background in:

- **biology**
- **chemistry**
- **anatomy and physiology**
- **entomology**

decomposing rotting or breaking down

larvae insects at the stage of development between eggs and adults

CHAPTER 4

ZOOKEEPERS

An adult elephant has bowel movements up to 10 times a day. It's the zookeeper's job to clean it up.

IN CAPTIVITY

An elephant strains. He is **constipated**. He shifts around on his feet in obvious discomfort. The zookeeper approaches the restless animal. Quickly she lifts the elephant's tail and reaches a gloved hand inside the animal's rectum. Grabbing hold of the large green bowel movement, she firmly pulls. In total she guides 2 m (7 feet) of smelly stool out of the sick animal's body. Elephants sometimes die of constipation. The zookeeper may have saved his life.

Zookeepers take care of animals in **captivity**. A big part of the job is keeping the animals and their living spaces clean. Animal droppings cannot pile up. They could make the animals sick. The zookeepers must get in and clean all the droppings. Some animals have small droppings, but elephant, hippopotamus and rhinoceros droppings can be very large. African elephants produce around 136 kg (300 pounds) of poo every day! Zookeepers sometimes just scoop the droppings and throw them away. Other times the zookeeper may need to look through them. A zookeeper can tell if an animal is sick from its droppings.

EDUCATION

Success as a zookeeper requires a strong background in:

- **zoology**
- **biology**
- **environmental science**

constipated when a person or animal is unable to release solid waste easily

captivity the condition of being confined or kept in a cage

IN THE WILD

Zoos do not only work with the animals within their walls. Many wild animals are at risk of dying out. Breeding programmes in zoos around the world can help. Zoos can provide safe places for breeding to help increase wild populations.

Zookeepers pair up mates and assist in delivering babies. Zookeepers must know how to guide animal birth and to spot any potential problems or dangers. They must be ready to rush in and help if something goes wrong. This can even include performing **CPR** on a newborn baby.

Once the babies grow up, zookeepers try to release the animals into the wild. Care must always be taken during the release process. The zookeepers must teach the animals how to survive on their own. This involves teaching them to hunt on their own and make shelter.

CPR short for cardiopulmonary resuscitation; CPR is a way of restarting a heart that has stopped beating

CALIFORNIA CONDORS

Some of the world's largest birds are also some of the most threatened. Large birds of prey, such as vultures and condors, suffer from habitat loss, decreasing food supply and poisoning.

Over the past 30 years, zoos and animal parks across Europe have worked hard to help these birds. Zoos such as the Prague Zoo breed vultures, hatch chicks and reintroduce the birds into the wild.

In 1982 only 22 California condors remained in North America. Multiple zoos helped create the California Condor Recovery Program. Condors are still endangered. But there are now more of them in the wild than in captivity.

Zookeepers around the world hope this is the beginning of a lasting comeback for these large birds of prey.

CHAPTER 5
HAZMAT DIVERS

When toxic materials spill or items need to be retrieved from **polluted** environments, hazardous materials (HAZMAT) divers are called. HAZMAT divers are trained to scuba dive into toxic places.

HAZMAT divers wear full diving helmets that weigh about 14 kg (30 pounds).

HAZMAT divers use special equipment when dealing with dangerous spills. They wear treated rubber suits with connected boots and gloves. The suits prevent dangerous material from seeping in. HAZMAT divers often use a giant underwater vacuum to suck up pollutants. After every dive, HAZMAT divers must be **decontaminated**. Team members spray divers with a special wash. They create the wash differently for each spill. They ensure that the wash contains no chemicals that could react with the pollutants in a harmful way.

HAZMAT divers must have engineering knowledge. Sometimes they repair leaky oil pipes on the ocean floor. When diving in polluted water, visibility is usually very low. HAZMAT divers often must blindly perform repairs on complicated machinery.

Chemistry is a big part of HAZMAT divers' jobs. Divers must know about the various toxins they encounter and why they are dangerous. They must know what to do if they are exposed and how to correctly dispose of the hazardous material.

EDUCATION

Success as a HAZMAT diver requires a strong background in:

- **chemistry**
- **engineering**
- **environmental science**

polluted unfit or harmful to living things

decontaminate to remove dirty or dangerous substances from a person, thing, or place

CHAPTER 6

WASTEWATER TREATMENT PLANT OPERATORS

The wastewater plant operator stands on a catwalk just 1 m (3 feet) above a vat of sewage. Using a long shovel-like tool, he scrapes floating scum from the surface of the water. The operator moves slowly to avoid splashing the sewage on himself. The hot summer's day strengthens the sewage smell.

Wastewater treatment plant operators might work with government agencies to monitor and maintain water quality.

Operators allow wastewater to settle in large vats. Scum made of grease, fat and paper products floats to the surface. The wastewater operator removes this layer of scum. The vats also filter out non-natural waste, such as metals, plastics and cloth. The plant operator must then clean this thick, smelly sludge out of the filters, often by hand.

Next, the water goes to large tubs where **bacteria** cleans it. These bacteria eat harmful microorganisms. The plant operator monitors the tubs, making sure the bacteria have enough food and air. The plant operator takes and tests samples of the sewage to make sure that the bacteria are doing their job.

Using knowledge of chemistry, the plant operator adds chlorine and other chemicals to further clean the water if needed. Then the water is finally ready to go back into the environment.

EDUCATION

Success as a wastewater treatment plant operator requires a strong background in:

- **chemistry**
- **engineering**
- **environmental science**

bacteria one-celled, tiny living things; some are helpful and some cause disease

CHAPTER 7
CAVE BIOLOGISTS

Footsteps echo off the rock walls. Narrow beams of light from several headlamps dart around. The scientists press onwards, feeling their way deeper into the earth. Down here in the extreme environment of caves, life is blossoming. These cave biologists came to study it.

Cave biologists must be comfortable going into tight spaces.

To get a glimpse of cave creatures, cave biologists have to get dirty. The insides of caves are covered in dirt, mud and droppings from bats and other animals. Cave biologists often crawl through very tight crevices covered in these substances. They may also wade through muck and water.

Many cave creatures have **evolved** to the constant darkness without a sense of sight. But their sense of smell works very well. Cave biologists sometimes use jars of strong-smelling cheese to attract the animals.

Cave biologists collect samples. After taking the samples back to the lab, they study the various forms of life that thrive in caves. Biologists hope that studying life in extreme environments like caves will help us find life on other planets.

evolve to change gradually

CHAPTER 8
OIL DRILL OPERATORS

The drill spins furiously as it rises from the ground. The drill head emerges, connected to a length of steel pipe. Three oil drill operators jump into action, locking the pipe into place and separating the drill. They do not step out of the way as red mud pours over their trousers and boots. They have a lot more pipe to lay before the sun goes down. Oil drill operators work long hours to get **fossil fuels** out of the earth.

Oil drill operators work at a drilling rig in Russia.

Drill operators guide large drill bits deep into the earth. The operator analyses the different layers of rock and soil that must be drilled through. Based on the **geology** of the site, the operator chooses an appropriate drill bit. Sometimes several different drill bits are needed as the drill passes through different layers of earth.

Drill operators must have mechanical engineering knowledge. Machines, such as water pumps and drills, sometimes break down. If this happens, the operator might take a machine apart, inspect it and repair it. Sometimes the machines just get dirty or clogged. The operator must clean out the mud, dirt, or grease before continuing work.

EDUCATION

Success as an oil drill operator requires a strong background in:

- **mechanical engineering**
- **mathematics**
- **earth science**

fossil fuel natural fuel formed from the remains of plants and animals; coal, oil and natural gas are fossil fuels

geology minerals, rocks and soil of an area

oil rig drill bit

CHAPTER 9
PALAEONTOLOGISTS

Orange dust swirls in the breeze. An eagle cries out from above. Down on the ground, several scientists are on their hands and knees. They carefully brush dirt from a fragment of bone. The bone, which once belonged to a dinosaur, has been buried for millions of years.

Palaeontologists dig up and study ancient **fossils**. These fossils can teach them about plants and animals of the past.

Palaeontologists study the remains of animals that lived thousands of years ago, such as the giant sloth.

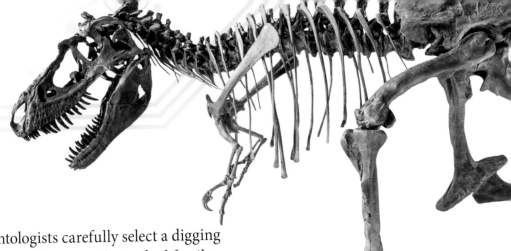

Palaeontologists carefully select a digging site. They might use radar to find fossils below the surface. Once a site is selected, palaeontologists start digging. This is when the job gets really dirty. Palaeontologists often must camp out in deserts or other remote locations for days or weeks at a time. At an **excavation** site, they will dig through **sedimentary rock** to find fossils. They use chisels, drills, picks and brushes to unearth and clean what they find.

Palaeontologists study fossils using advanced technology. They use CT scanners. CT scanners are like large X-ray machines. A scan of a dinosaur's skull can tell palaeontologists about its brain, sense of smell, sight and hearing. Palaeontologists love finding fossilized dung. It can tell them what a dinosaur ate and how its digestive system worked.

EDUCATION

Success as a palaeontologist requires a strong background in:

- **biology**
- **geology**

fossil remains or traces of an animal or a plant, preserved as rock

excavation digging in the earth

sedimentary rock rock formed by layers of rocks, sand, or clay that have been pressed together

CHAPTER 10
MANURE INSPECTORS

Squish! No one likes stepping in poo. But that is part of the job of a manure inspector. Manure inspectors have one of the dirtiest jobs around. They walk through animal manure, collect samples and inspect manure storage bins.

Manure inspectors monitor farms and make sure manure is handled safely. They want to see where manure is collected and stored. If the area is not properly sealed, bacteria could leak into the groundwater and pollute well water or water used to water crops. Bacteria could also contaminate the manure, which is often used as fertilizer for crops.

Fresh cow manure is about 70 to 85 per cent water.

horse manure

The inspectors test the manure for harmful bacteria, such as salmonella and E. coli. To do this, they wear protective suits, rubber boots, goggles and masks. Sometimes they have to walk through large piles of manure to get several different samples. They write reports on their findings. Then manure inspectors recommend action to be taken to protect people and the environment.

EDUCATION

Success as a manure inspector requires a strong background in:

- **biology**
- **chemistry**
- **animal science**

STEAM FACT

A full-grown dairy cow produces about 52 kg (115 pounds) of manure every day.

GLOSSARY

bacteria one-celled, tiny living things; some are helpful and some cause disease

captivity condition of being confined or kept in a cage

constipated when a person or animal is unable to release solid waste easily

CPR short for cardiopulmonary resuscitation; CPR is a way of restarting a heart that has stopped beating

decomposing rotting or breaking down

decontaminate to remove dirty or dangerous substances from a person, thing, or place

evolve to change gradually

excavation digging in the earth

fossil remains or traces of an animal or a plant, preserved as rock

fossil fuel natural fuel formed from the remains of plants and animals; coal, oil and natural gas are fossil fuels

geologist person who studies rocks

geology minerals, rocks and soil of an area

larvae insects at the stage of development between eggs and adults

oesophagus long tube that carries food from the mouth to the stomach

polluted something that is dirty or unsafe

rectal having to do with the rectum, the tube that releases solid waste

scope tool a doctor uses to listen to or see inside a person's body

sedimentary rock rock formed by layers of rocks, sand, or clay that have been pressed together

stools bodily waste that comes out of the anus

surveying measuring land in order to make a plan for how to use it

FIND OUT MORE

BOOKS

Crime Scene Clues (Zoom in On), Richard Spilsbury (Wayland, 2015)

Forensic Secrets (Amazing Crime Scene Science), John Townsend (Franklin Watts, 2012)

Fossils, David Ward (Dorling Kindersley, 2010)

WEBSITES

www.myworldofwork.co.uk/my-career-options/job-profiles/zookeeper
Have a look at this website to find out more about being a zookeeper.

nationalcareersservice.direct.gov.uk
Use this website to get advice about training and careers.

successatschool.org
More helpful advice can be found on this national careers website.

INDEX